LEADING
PLCs
AT WORK®
Districtwide

PLAN BOOK

ROBERT EAKER   JANEL KEATING
MIKE HAGADONE   MEAGAN RHOADES

If found, please return this plan book to:
Name _____
School _____
Room _____
Address _____
Telephone _____ Cell phone _____
Email _____

Emergency Contact Information
Police _____
Fire _____
Doctor _____
Other _____
_____
_____

Solution Tree | Press a division of
Solution Tree

555 North Morton Street
Bloomington, IN 47404
800.733.6786 (toll free) / 812.336.7700
FAX: 812.336.7790
email: info@SolutionTree.com
SolutionTree.com

Visit **go.SolutionTree.com/PLCbooks** to download the free reproducibles in this book.
Printed in the United States of America

Library of Congress Cataloging-in-Publication Data

Names: Eaker, Robert E., author. | Hagadone, Mike, author. | Keating, Janel, author. | Rhoades, Meagan, author.
Title: Leading PLCS at work districtwide plan book / Robert Eaker, Mike Hagadone, Janel Keating, Meagan Rhoades.
Description: Bloomington, IN : Solution Tree Press, [2021] | Includes bibliographical references and index.
Identifiers: LCCN 2020031269 (print) | LCCN 2020031270 (ebook) | ISBN 9781952812170 (paperback) | ISBN 9781952812187 (ebook)
Subjects: LCSH: Educational planning. | Professional learning communities.
Classification: LCC LC71.2 .E25 2021 (print) | LCC LC71.2 (ebook) | DDC 371.2/07--dc23
LC record available at https://lccn.loc.gov/2020031269
LC ebook record available at https://lccn.loc.gov/2020031270

Solution Tree
Jeffrey C. Jones, CEO
Edmund M. Ackerman, President

Solution Tree Press
President and Publisher: Douglas M. Rife
Associate Publisher: Sarah Payne-Mills
Art Director: Rian Anderson
Managing Production Editor: Kendra Slayton
Copy Chief: Jessi Finn
Senior Production Editor: Suzanne Kraszewski
Content Development Specialist: Amy Rubenstein
Copy Editor: Kate St. Ives
Proofreader: Jessi Finn
Text and Cover Designer: Rian Anderson
Editorial Assistants: Sarah Ludwig and Elijah Oates

Table of Contents

Reproducible pages are in italics.

Visit **go.SolutionTree.com/PLCbooks**
to download the free reproducibles in this book.

Visit **go.SolutionTree.com/PLCbooks**
to download the free reproducibles in this book.

About the Authors

Robert Eaker, EdD, is professor emeritus at Middle Tennessee State University, where he also served as dean of the College of Education and later as interim executive vice president and provost. Dr. Eaker is a former fellow with the National Center for Effective Schools Research and Development.

Dr. Eaker has written widely on the issues of effective teaching, effective schools, helping teachers use research findings, and high expectations for student achievement, and has coauthored (with Richard DuFour and Rebecca DuFour) numerous books and other resources on the topic of reculturing schools and school districts into professional learning communities (PLCs).

For over four decades, Dr. Eaker has served as a consultant to school districts throughout North America and has been a frequent speaker at state, regional, and national meetings.

To learn more about Dr. Eaker, visit AllThingsPLC (www.allthingsplc.info).

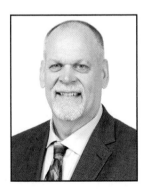

Mike Hagadone, MEd, served as the assistant superintendent of White River School District in Washington State until his retirement in 2020. With forty years of experience, he is a former teacher, assistant principal, principal, and director of secondary education.

During his tenure as principal at White River High School in Buckley, Washington, the school was recognized as a Washington Achievement Award Winner (2011) and a School of Distinction (2012). White River High School was designated as a Model PLC by Solution Tree in 2015.

Janel Keating, MEd, is the superintendent of the White River School District in Buckley, Washington. An accomplished educator with more than thirty years of experience, Janel has served as an elementary and middle school teacher, elementary principal, director of student learning, and deputy superintendent. For eight years, Janel had the privilege of being the principal of Mountain Meadow Elementary School in Buckley, Washington. During her time there, Mountain Meadow was recognized as one of the highest academically performing elementary schools in the state (2004 and 2006). Mountain Meadow is currently the highest performing of nearly 180 elementary schools in Pierce County and a 2020 DuFour Award finalist. Janel has written numerous books and articles on leadership and school improvement.

Meagan Rhoades is the district assessment coordinator in White River School District in Buckley, Washington. She has worked in this district for more than twenty years, starting in the district as a substitute paraeducator, then working as a building secretary, and then moving to the district office and working in the technology department.

Meagan has presented and copresented at numerous conferences. She has also served as a consultant for several school districts and has been a cowriter for Solution Tree blogs and the website AllThingsPLC (www.allthingsplc.info).

To book Robert Eaker, Mike Hagadone, Janel Keating, or Meagan Rhoades for professional development, contact pd@SolutionTree.com.

PART 1
About This Plan Book

Districtwide Planning

There is a huge difference between hoping for, or even being committed to, school improvement and *planning* for school improvement. Planning requires action. It is the process through which leaders embed core values in the work at the district, school, and team levels. Planning institutionalizes what schools care most about. Planning is a leader's way of proclaiming, "This is so important we are going to collaboratively develop a plan to ensure it gets done—on time and with a high level of quality."

At the most basic level, effective planning is a collaborative effort. There is a strong correlation between the quality of collaboration that goes into the planning process and the quality of the plan itself. As Debra Sells and I (2016) point out, "Effective collaboration in, effective plans out!" (p. 116). The fact is, people who have no, or little, say in the development of plans have very little, if any, commitment to ensuring the plan succeeds.

Although effective planning is a collaborative process, it is more than a mere averaging of opinions. Plans must be relevant and meaningful. Effective leaders ensure relevance and meaning through consistently connecting the plan to the *why*—why each goal is important and why it contributes to the district's vision for the future and mission of high levels of learning for all students. A single initial reference to the why is never enough; effective leaders frequently connect the planning process back to the why question in multiple ways.

Planning, to a great extent, involves working backward. That is, once the goal of the plan is determined and the date for achieving the goal is set, planners must identify the major tasks that are involved in reaching the goal. (This process of planning from the end to the start is often referred to as performance evaluation review technique [PERT] charting, a process developed by the Navy in the early 1950s [Owens, 1970].) Simply put, each major task must be completed prior to the deadline for goal attainment. This leads to ease in identifying the associated activities that must be accomplished prior to completing each major task. The process of working backward and identifying major tasks and due dates, along with essential activities and completion dates, provides a rational collaborative process that focuses on the right things for the right reasons.

After developing major tasks, activities, and timelines, it is helpful to depict the plan in a way that is visual—this way, everyone can see what needs to be done and when. Effective planning must be transparent and monitored on a frequent and timely basis. Additionally, people need to see how things connect—how various activities and tasks connect to a larger goal.

This plan book assists school and district leaders as they implement the Professional Learning Communities at Work (PLC) process in their buildings and across the district. It guides educators in knowing what to do when and connects building and team work with district goals while also providing critical planning and organizing space for leaders to focus on all the important work in a PLC. The goal of this resource is to move leaders from hoping for school improvement to taking action by planning for improvement.

—Robert Eaker

How to Use This Plan Book

As leaders in education, we often feel that the profession—and life in general—gets incrementally busier and more complex each year. Every issue we need to consider and every decision we have to make reduces our available cognitive load for a given day. An effective planning process helps to reduce the load we are carrying. It creates a written record of what we have done during the year, which makes it simple to review what worked well and what did not—what you want, or need, to change and what you can systematize. Ideally, a good planner helps to free your brain for the creative problem solving that pushes the work of your school or district forward. A well-crafted plan provides more than just an outline for upcoming days and weeks. It also creates a written record of accomplishments and a road map for future planning.

In this planner, you will find a variety of tools to lead your school or district PLC organized by month and by week. The following elements appear in the month-by-month planner pages that appear in parts 2 and 3 of this plan book.

PLC Work

The planner includes a monthly list of PLC tasks for you to incorporate into your planning. These tasks are framed around the four critical questions of a PLC (DuFour, DuFour, Eaker, Many, & Mattos, 2016).

1. What do we want students to know and be able to do?
2. How will we know if each student has learned it?
3. How will we respond if some students do not learn it?
4. How will we extend the learning for students who have demonstrated proficiency?

These PLC Work sections provide a checklist of tasks to guide your work. The companion book to this plan book, *Leading PLCs at Work® Districtwide: From Boardroom to Classroom* (Eaker, Hagadone, Keating, & Rhoades, 2021), provides in-depth examination of the work of district and school leaders in a PLC and will support you in this work. It also contains many reproducibles that will assist you in your work throughout the year.

You will find frequent references in the PLC Work sections to response to intervention (RTI) and multitiered system of support (MTSS). The book *Taking Action: A Handbook for RTI at Work*™ (Buffum, Mattos, & Malone, 2018) supports the detailed work around implementing a system of intervention for students who struggle and includes many tools and reproducibles to support your work.

Monthly Management and Building Work

As you begin your planning, you will see a section for monthly management work. This section outlines the tasks that every building needs to accomplish, such as benchmark testing, planning events, checking in with new staff, planning assemblies for the year, and establishing student growth goals. There is also a place to add building work. These are tasks that are specific to your building and might include things like an art auction, a family reading night, or STEAM events. This section also contains a monthly calendar and note page to assist you in your planning efforts.

Weekly Planner

Each weekly planner has planning pages that include the following sections.

- **Complete task list:** Use this section to write a list of tasks for the week.
- **Must-do list:** This is a place to note high-priority tasks, phone calls, and emails.
- **Ten-minute tasks:** These tasks are items you can quickly check off your to-do list when you have several free moments, such as while you are waiting for a meeting to start or when you arrive in the morning.
- **Classrooms check-ins:** List which classrooms and teachers you plan to check in on during the week and when.
- **Feedback and follow-up**: List any feedback you plan to give or follow-up you plan to pursue.
- **Celebrations of success:** Note what and who you plan to celebrate this week.
- **Positive notes and parent connections:** List positive notes to send and positive parent connections to make. We highly recommend including this element in your planning so it's not forgotten.
- **Self-care plan:** Use this space to answer the question, How will I take care of myself this week? Note what you plan to read and listen to, for example, or when you will exercise or call a friend.

- **Notes and big projects ongoing or upcoming:** This section has room for notes along with space for big projects that you need to keep at the front of your mind, either ongoing or upcoming.

My Monthly Reflections

In the monthly reflection tool, you can reflect on the following things.

- Accomplishments
- What went well
- Lessons learned
- What to change
- Systems to put in place that would make this month go smoother next year
- What to simplify or do away with to improve this month next year

District Leadership Meeting Commitments

Use this tool during and after district leadership meetings. Detail what commitments you have made in your building that align with the learning from the meeting and district and building goals. What is your plan for the work that will happen at your building leadership meetings based on those commitments? What products will you share at the next meeting? What is your evidence of success?

Tools

This book includes tools for you to use in your personal and professional planning. The Midyear Reflection tool includes prompts for leader reflection on the first half of the school year, from August through December. The End-of-Year Reflections tool provides prompts for reflection on the entire school year. The "Project Planner" reproducible provides a place to organize your thoughts and steps during project planning, as well as create a detailed record to refer back to in the future. The "Setting Professional and Personal Goals" reproducible and the "Goal-Setting Worksheet" reproducible help you organize your goals—understanding your motivation, how you will measure them, what success will look like, and how you will make adjustments along the way.

In *Keeping on Your Feet*, Gene Sharratt (2002) writes of the importance of knowing the difference between the rubber balls and the glass balls in our work: "When rubber balls fall, they bounce back. When glass balls fall, they shatter" (p. 12). From a leadership perspective, the glass balls are the essential actions for a leader; without these actions, irreversible damage will occur. In contrast, the rubber balls can be caught on the rebound with little to no harm done. This plan book is designed to help you focus on the glass balls, and create systems for dealing with the rubber balls.

U.S. Holidays and Observances

Add the celebrations you want to recognize to your calendar. You may have local or state celebrations to add as well.

September
- Labor Day
- International Literacy Day
- National Arts in Education Week
- National School Backpack Awareness Day
- Talk Like a Pirate Day
- National Grandparents Day

October
- National Bullying Prevention Month
- Maintenance and Custodian Appreciation Day
- National Fire Prevention Week
- Child Health Day
- International Walk to School Day
- National School Lunch Week
- Make-a-Difference Day

November
- Set Clocks Back Day
- Veterans Day
- National School Psychologist Week
- American Education Week
- Educational Support Professionals Day
- National Parent Involvement Day
- Substitute Educators Day

December
- National Inclusive Schools Week

January
- School Board Appreciation Month
- National Mentoring Month
- Martin Luther King Jr. Day
- Holocaust Remembrance Week

February
- National School Counseling Week
- National PTA Founders Day
- National FFA Week

March
- National Nutrition Month
- Social Work Month
- National Music in Our Schools Month
- Theater in Our Schools Month
- Youth Art Month
- NEA Read Across America Day
- Set Clocks Ahead Day
- National School Breakfast Week
- Pi Day
- Classified Employee Appreciation Week

April
- School Library Month
- World Autism Awareness Month
- International Children's Book Day
- National Library Week
- National Librarian Appreciation Day
- Administrative Professionals Week
- National Student Leadership Week
- Public School Volunteer Week
- Earth Day

May
- National Physical Fitness Month
- Educational Bosses Week
- Teacher Appreciation Week
- National Teacher Appreciation Day
- National Children's Book Week
- National Bike to School Day
- School Lunch Hero Day
- Mother's Day
- National School Nurse Day
- Employee Health and Fitness Day
- Memorial Day

June
- Zoo and Aquarium Month
- National Donut Day
- Father's Day

July
- Independence Day
- International Friendship Day

August
- National Truancy Prevention Month
- Book Lovers Day
- International Youth Day
- Women's Equality Day

Reculturing schools to become professional learning communities is hard work. The issue is not simply a question of *knowing* but of *doing*, and beyond that, of *leading*—of will. There is little doubt that professional learning community concepts and practices can be a powerful force for improving school districts and thus the learning levels of students. But becoming a professional learning community requires action, courage, risk taking, and persistence. We will never change the traditional culture of school districts by seeking safe, calm harbors. We must set sail into a sea of uncertainty, knowing full well that storms and rough seas lie ahead. But we must set sail, simply because the stakes are so high. These are *our* children, our future. They deserve to be educated at high levels, not merely required to attend school.

So, for those who are committed to leaving safe harbors and calm seas and setting sail to reculturing schools into high-performing professional learning communities, it is our sincere hope that the following ideas, suggestions, and resources will assist you on your journey to become a high-performing professional learning community, because the journey is inherently worthwhile. Our desire is that each reader, after reviewing the year ahead, will be motivated to declare, "We can do this!" and ask, "Why not *us*? Why not *now*?"

—Robert Eaker and Janel Keating

PART 2

Planning Pages

JULY AND AUGUST

JULY AND AUGUST PLC WORK

- Attend administrative retreat.
- Hold administrative meetings to discuss nuts and bolts (for example, annual human resources policy updates and training).
- Attend Professional Learning Communities at Work Institute or provide and share district training.
- Hold leadership team meeting and training; the work and information from this meeting will flow to the collaborative grade-level and content teams.
  - Review student achievement data.
  - Establish school SMART goals (Conzemius & O'Neill, 2014).
  - Write norms and accountability protocols.
  - Read chapter 9, "Addressing Conflict and Celebrating in a Professional Learning Community," in *Learning by Doing* (DuFour et al., 2016, pp. 211–232).
  - Create collaboration calendar.
  - Revisit collaboration expectations and read "Stomping Out PLC Lite" (Keating & Rhoades, 2019).
  - Revisit collective commitments and read "A Shift in School Culture" (Eaker & Keating, 2008).
  - Schedule monthly leadership team meetings.
  - Review scope and sequence of essential standards.
  - Update unit plans based on state assessment data.
  - Identify data that will be reviewed monthly based on the essential standards.
- Review student achievement data from the previous year with staff to ensure specific students receive time and support immediately.
- Revisit master schedule and ask whether it reflects what you value.
  - Collaboration time
  - Additional time, support, and extensions (Tiers 2 and 3)
  - Uninterrupted blocks of time for core instruction
- Schedule MTSS, RTI, and PBIS meetings.
- Plan opening learning days with staff.
- Review the professional development plan.
- Review grading and reporting expectations with staff.
- Plan for and communicate expectations for singletons.
- Plan for schoolwide social-emotional learning focus.

NOTES

_____

_____

_____

July and August Management Work

☐ Finalize hiring.

☐ Walk through the school with the plant supervisor or custodian.

☐ Draft and send welcome-back letter to staff.

☐ Draft and send welcome letter to families.

☐ Call the families of new students to welcome them.

☐ Meet with PTA or PTO board.

☐ Plan and host open house, back-to-school night, or other welcome activity.

☐ Make master schedule adjustments.

☐ Ensure all schedules are in place.

- Special education and 504s

- Intervention and extension

- Paraeducator

- Educational assistants

- Specialists

- Assessments (state, ACT, SAT, PSAT, AP, and so on)

☐ Complete learning improvement plan with district leadership team. (See *Leading PLCs at Work Districtwide: From Boardroom to Classroom* [Eaker et al., 2021] to learn more about PLC implementation districtwide.)

☐ Revisit PLC implementation plan

July and August Building Work

☐

☐

☐

☐

☐

☐

NOTES

JULY

Sunday	Monday	Tuesday	Wednesday	Thursday	Friday	Saturday

AUGUST

Sunday	Monday	Tuesday	Wednesday	Thursday	Friday	Saturday

NOTES

MONDAY

TUESDAY

WEDNESDAY

THURSDAY

FRIDAY

COMPLETE TASK LIST

- ☐
- ☐
- ☐
- ☐
- ☐
- ☐
- ☐
- ☐
- ☐
- ☐
- ☐
- ☐
- ☐
- ☐
- ☐

NOTES

MUST-DO LIST

TEN-MINUTE TASKS

Phone Calls

Emails

Classrooms Check-Ins

Feedback and Follow-Up

Celebrations of Success

Positive Note

Positive Parent Connections

Self-Care Plan

Big Projects Ongoing or Upcoming

DATE _____

MONDAY

TUESDAY

WEDNESDAY

THURSDAY

FRIDAY

COMPLETE TASK LIST

☐
☐
☐
☐
☐
☐
☐
☐
☐
☐
☐
☐
☐
☐
☐

NOTES

_____
_____
_____
_____
_____
_____
_____
_____
_____

MUST-DO LIST

TEN-MINUTE TASKS

Phone Calls

Emails

Classrooms Check-Ins

Feedback and Follow-Up

Celebrations of Success

Positive Note

Positive Parent Connections

Self-Care Plan

Big Projects Ongoing or Upcoming

DATE _____

MONDAY

TUESDAY

WEDNESDAY

THURSDAY

FRIDAY

COMPLETE TASK LIST

☐
☐
☐
☐
☐
☐
☐
☐
☐
☐
☐
☐
☐
☐
☐
☐

NOTES

MUST-DO LIST

TEN-MINUTE TASKS

Phone Calls

Emails

Classrooms Check-Ins

Feedback and Follow-Up

Celebrations of Success

Positive Note

Positive Parent Connections

Self-Care Plan

Big Projects Ongoing or Upcoming

DATE _____

MONDAY

TUESDAY

WEDNESDAY

THURSDAY

FRIDAY

COMPLETE TASK LIST

☐
☐
☐
☐
☐
☐
☐
☐
☐
☐
☐
☐
☐
☐
☐

NOTES

_____
_____
_____
_____
_____
_____
_____
_____

MUST-DO LIST

TEN-MINUTE TASKS

Phone Calls

Emails

Classrooms Check-Ins

Feedback and Follow-Up

Celebrations of Success

Positive Note

Positive Parent Connections

Self-Care Plan

Big Projects Ongoing or Upcoming

DATE _____

MONDAY

TUESDAY

WEDNESDAY

THURSDAY

FRIDAY

COMPLETE TASK LIST

☐
☐
☐
☐
☐
☐
☐
☐
☐
☐
☐
☐
☐
☐
☐
☐

NOTES

MUST-DO LIST

TEN-MINUTE TASKS

Phone Calls

Emails

Classrooms Check-Ins

Feedback and Follow-Up

Celebrations of Success

Positive Note

Positive Parent Connections

Self-Care Plan

Big Projects Ongoing or Upcoming

MY MONTHLY REFLECTIONS

ACCOMPLISHMENTS

WHAT WENT WELL

LESSONS LEARNED

WHAT TO CHANGE

Are there systems I can put in place that would make this month go smoother next year?

What is something I can simplify or do away with to improve this month next year?

DISTRICT LEADERSHIP MEETING COMMITMENTS

Use this tool to document commitments you or your building leadership team are making based on the work at this month's district leadership meeting.

Building leadership team meeting: _____ **Date:** _____

Commitments based on principal or building leadership team work:

Plan for next steps or work for building leadership team meeting:

Evidence of commitments:

SEPTEMBER

"

The leader's role in a
professional learning
community is to promote,
protect, and defend the
school's vision and values
and to confront behavior
that is inconsistent with the
school's vision and values.

**—Robert Eaker, Richard
DuFour, and Rebecca DuFour**

SEPTEMBER PLC WORK

- Review scope and sequence of essential standards by grade level and content area.
- Set teacher observation schedule to align with essential standards in content areas and grade levels.
- Review staff expectations surrounding collaboration.
- Visit collaborative meetings to observe evidence of the following.
  - Norms, accountability protocols, and collective commitments
  - Essential standards and learning targets
  - Data or student work at the team table
  - Discussion surrounding where students did well and instructional strategies that helped students
  - Discussion surrounding additional time, support, and extensions
  - Discussion surrounding the next targets and instructional strategies and formative assessment
- Review products from weekly collaborative meeting with administrative team, instructional coaches, and teachers on special assignment.
- Analyze benchmark assessment results in English language arts and mathematics.
- Observe core instruction (Tier 1).
- Observe Tier 2 intervention. Is there a direct connection to core instruction (Tier 1)?
- Observe Tier 3 intervention. What universal skills are being taught using a research-based curriculum? Review the progress-monitoring data. Remember the following: Tier 3 students receive all three tiers of instruction.
- Craft school-improvement plan.
- Plan team learning celebration. Celebrate the things you value for students and staff.
- Plan and hold leadership team meeting.
- Determine learning focus of the staff meeting aligned with the district leadership team meeting and the building leadership team meeting held last month, and the school-improvement plan.
- Analyze data from next end-of-unit assessment and schedule vertical articulation team meetings based on data.
- Provide data report to the school board.
- Plan for schoolwide social-emotional learning focus.

NOTES

September Management Work

- [ ] Host back-to-school night and curriculum night.
- [ ] Check in with new staff members.
- [ ] Conduct benchmark testing.
- [ ] Hold staff meeting.
- [ ] Hold PTA or PTO meeting.
- [ ] Conduct bus safety drills.
- [ ] Review parent drop-off and pick-up information.
- [ ] Review emergency procedures and schedule drills.
- [ ] Plan for ongoing events.
    - Assemblies to include student achievement
    - Student-of-the-month awards (school, Rotary, Kiwanis, and so on)
    - Field trips
- [ ] Meet with substitute teachers.
- [ ] Establish student growth goals.

September Building Work

- [ ]
- [ ]
- [ ]
- [ ]
- [ ]
- [ ]
- [ ]

NOTES

SEPTEMBER

Sunday	Monday	Tuesday	Wednesday	Thursday	Friday	Saturday

September

NOTES

_____

_____

_____

_____

_____

_____

_____

_____

_____

_____

_____

_____

_____

_____

_____

DATE _____

September

MONDAY

TUESDAY

WEDNESDAY

THURSDAY

FRIDAY

COMPLETE TASK LIST

- ☐
- ☐
- ☐
- ☐
- ☐
- ☐
- ☐
- ☐
- ☐
- ☐
- ☐
- ☐
- ☐
- ☐
- ☐
- ☐

NOTES

_____
_____
_____
_____
_____
_____
_____
_____
_____

MUST-DO LIST

TEN-MINUTE TASKS

Phone Calls

Emails

Classrooms Check-Ins

Feedback and Follow-Up

Celebrations of Success

Positive Note

Positive Parent Connections

Self-Care Plan

Big Projects Ongoing or Upcoming

DATE _____

MONDAY

TUESDAY

WEDNESDAY

THURSDAY

FRIDAY

COMPLETE TASK LIST

☐
☐
☐
☐
☐
☐
☐
☐
☐
☐
☐
☐
☐
☐
☐
☐

NOTES

_____
_____
_____
_____
_____
_____
_____
_____
_____

MUST-DO LIST

TEN-MINUTE TASKS

Phone Calls

Emails

Classrooms Check-Ins

Feedback and Follow-Up

Celebrations of Success

Positive Note

Positive Parent Connections

Self-Care Plan

Big Projects Ongoing or Upcoming

DATE _____

September

MONDAY

TUESDAY

WEDNESDAY

THURSDAY

FRIDAY

COMPLETE TASK LIST

- [ ]
- [ ]
- [ ]
- [ ]
- [ ]
- [ ]
- [ ]
- [ ]
- [ ]
- [ ]
- [ ]
- [ ]
- [ ]
- [ ]
- [ ]

NOTES

_____
_____
_____
_____
_____
_____
_____
_____
_____

MUST-DO LIST

TEN-MINUTE TASKS

Phone Calls

Emails

Classrooms Check-Ins

Feedback and Follow-Up

Celebrations of Success

Positive Note

Positive Parent Connections

Self-Care Plan

Big Projects Ongoing or Upcoming

DATE _____

September

MONDAY

TUESDAY

WEDNESDAY

THURSDAY

FRIDAY

COMPLETE TASK LIST

☐
☐
☐
☐
☐
☐
☐
☐
☐
☐
☐
☐
☐
☐
☐

NOTES

_____
_____
_____
_____
_____
_____
_____
_____

MUST-DO LIST

TEN-MINUTE TASKS

Phone Calls

Emails

Classrooms Check-Ins

Feedback and Follow-Up

Celebrations of Success

Positive Note

Positive Parent Connections

Self-Care Plan

Big Projects Ongoing or Upcoming

DATE _____

MONDAY

TUESDAY

WEDNESDAY

THURSDAY

FRIDAY

COMPLETE TASK LIST

- ☐
- ☐
- ☐
- ☐
- ☐
- ☐
- ☐
- ☐
- ☐
- ☐
- ☐
- ☐
- ☐
- ☐
- ☐
- ☐

NOTES

_____
_____
_____
_____
_____
_____
_____
_____

MUST-DO LIST

TEN-MINUTE TASKS

Phone Calls

Emails

Classrooms Check-Ins

Feedback and Follow-Up

Celebrations of Success

Positive Note

Positive Parent Connections

Self-Care Plan

Big Projects Ongoing or Upcoming

MY MONTHLY REFLECTIONS

ACCOMPLISHMENTS

WHAT WENT WELL

LESSONS LEARNED

WHAT TO CHANGE

Are there systems I can put in place that would make this month go smoother next year?

What is something I can simplify or do away with to improve this month next year?

DISTRICT LEADERSHIP MEETING COMMITMENTS

Use this tool to document commitments you or your building leadership team are making based on the work at this month's district leadership meeting.

Building leadership team meeting: _____   **Date:** _____

September

Commitments based on principal or building leadership team work:

Plan for next steps or work for building leadership team meeting:

Evidence of commitments:

OCTOBER

> "
>
> School leaders must do more than deliver curriculum documents to teachers to ensure all students have an opportunity to master the same essential learning. They must engage every teacher in a collaborative process to study, to clarify, and most importantly, to commit to teaching the curriculum.
>
> **—Richard DuFour, Rebecca DuFour, Robert Eaker, and Thomas Many**

OCTOBER PLC WORK

- Ensure teacher observation schedule will align with essential standards in content areas and grade levels.
- Visit collaborative meetings to observe evidence of the following.
  - Norms, accountability protocols, and collective commitments
  - Essential standards and learning targets
  - Data or student work at the team table
  - Discussion surrounding where students did well and instructional strategies that helped students
  - Discussion surrounding additional time, support, and extensions
  - Discussion surrounding the next targets and instructional strategies and formative assessment
- Review products from weekly collaborative meeting with administrative team, instructional coaches, and teachers on special assignment.
- Observe core instruction (Tier 1).
- Observe Tier 2 intervention. Is there a direct connection to core instruction (Tier 1)?
- Observe Tier 3 intervention. What universal skills are being taught using a research-based curriculum? Review the progress-monitoring data.
- Plan and hold team learning celebration. Celebrate the things you value for students and staff.
- Plan and hold leadership team meeting.
- Determine learning focus of the staff meeting aligned with the district leadership team meeting and the building leadership team meeting held last month, and the school-improvement plan.
- Analyze data from next end-of-unit assessment and schedule vertical articulation team meetings based on data.
- Plan and hold MTSS/RTI and PBIS meeting.
- Plan for schoolwide social-emotional learning focus.

NOTES

October Management Work

- [ ] Hold staff meeting.
- [ ] Hold PTA or PTO meeting.
- [ ] Review emergency procedures and hold drills.
- [ ] Conduct parent, teacher, and student conferences.
- [ ] Identify who each administrator is in charge of evaluating (for schools with an administrative team).
- [ ] Give learning improvement presentation to school board.

October Building Work

- [ ]
- [ ]
- [ ]
- [ ]
- [ ]
- [ ]
- [ ]
- [ ]

NOTES

OCTOBER

Sunday	Monday	Tuesday	Wednesday	Thursday	Friday	Saturday

October

NOTES

DATE _____

MONDAY

TUESDAY

WEDNESDAY

THURSDAY

FRIDAY

COMPLETE TASK LIST

☐
☐
☐
☐
☐
☐
☐
☐
☐
☐
☐
☐
☐
☐
☐
☐
☐

NOTES

MUST-DO LIST

TEN-MINUTE TASKS

Phone Calls

Emails

Classrooms Check-Ins

Feedback and Follow-Up

Celebrations of Success

Positive Note

Positive Parent Connections

Self-Care Plan

Big Projects Ongoing or Upcoming

DATE _____

MONDAY

TUESDAY

WEDNESDAY

THURSDAY

FRIDAY

COMPLETE TASK LIST

- [ ]
- [ ]
- [ ]
- [ ]
- [ ]
- [ ]
- [ ]
- [ ]
- [ ]
- [ ]
- [ ]
- [ ]
- [ ]
- [ ]
- [ ]

NOTES

_____
_____
_____
_____
_____
_____
_____
_____
_____

MUST-DO LIST

TEN-MINUTE TASKS

Phone Calls

Emails

Classrooms Check-Ins

Feedback and Follow-Up

Celebrations of Success

Positive Note

Positive Parent Connections

Self-Care Plan

Big Projects Ongoing or Upcoming

DATE _____

MONDAY

TUESDAY

WEDNESDAY

THURSDAY

FRIDAY

COMPLETE TASK LIST

- [ ]
- [ ]
- [ ]
- [ ]
- [ ]
- [ ]
- [ ]
- [ ]
- [ ]
- [ ]
- [ ]
- [ ]
- [ ]
- [ ]
- [ ]

NOTES

_____
_____
_____
_____
_____
_____
_____
_____
_____

MUST-DO LIST

TEN-MINUTE TASKS

Phone Calls

Emails

Classrooms Check-Ins

Feedback and Follow-Up

Celebrations of Success

Positive Note

Positive Parent Connections

Self-Care Plan

Big Projects Ongoing or Upcoming

DATE _____

MONDAY

TUESDAY

WEDNESDAY

THURSDAY

FRIDAY

COMPLETE TASK LIST

☐
☐
☐
☐
☐
☐
☐
☐
☐
☐
☐
☐
☐
☐
☐
☐

NOTES

MUST-DO LIST

TEN-MINUTE TASKS

Phone Calls

Emails

Classrooms Check-Ins

Feedback and Follow-Up

Celebrations of Success

Positive Note

Positive Parent Connections

Self-Care Plan

Big Projects Ongoing or Upcoming

DATE _____

MONDAY

TUESDAY

WEDNESDAY

THURSDAY

FRIDAY

COMPLETE TASK LIST

☐
☐
☐
☐
☐
☐
☐
☐
☐
☐
☐
☐
☐
☐
☐
☐

NOTES

MUST-DO LIST

TEN-MINUTE TASKS

October

Phone Calls

Emails

Classrooms Check-Ins

Feedback and Follow-Up

Celebrations of Success

Positive Note

Positive Parent Connections

Self-Care Plan

Big Projects Ongoing or Upcoming

MY MONTHLY REFLECTIONS

October

ACCOMPLISHMENTS

WHAT WENT WELL

LESSONS LEARNED

WHAT TO CHANGE

Are there systems I can put in place that would make this month go smoother next year?

What is something I can simplify or do away with to improve this month next year?

DISTRICT LEADERSHIP MEETING COMMITMENTS

Use this tool to document commitments you or your building leadership team are making based on the work at this month's district leadership meeting.

Building leadership team meeting: _____ **Date:** _____

October

Commitments based on principal or building leadership team work:

Plan for next steps or work for building leadership team meeting:

Evidence of commitments:

NOVEMBER

"

Leaders can't be afraid of powerful verbs such as *expect*, *require*, and *support*. They often wonder if it's possible to expect and require and still build positive relationships. District leaders must confidently state, "We're going to expect, require, and support our staff to do the work of ensuring high levels of learning for all students by embedding the concepts and practices of a PLC in our day-to-day work." We live by this motto: "Relentless pressure, gracefully applied."

—Robert Eaker, Mike Hagadone, Janel Keating, and Meagan Rhoades

NOVEMBER PLC WORK

- Ensure teacher observation schedule will align with essential standards in content areas and grade levels.
- Visit collaborative meetings to observe evidence of the following.
  - Norms, accountability protocols, and collective commitments
  - Essential standards and learning targets
  - Data or student work at the team table
  - Discussion surrounding where students did well and instructional strategies that helped students
  - Discussion surrounding additional time, support, and extensions
  - Discussion surrounding the next targets and instructional strategies and formative assessment
- Review products from weekly collaborative meeting with administrative team, instructional coaches, and teachers on special assignment.
- Observe core instruction (Tier 1).
- Observe Tier 2 intervention. Is there a direct connection to core instruction?
- Observe Tier 3 intervention. What universal skills are being taught using a research-based curriculum? Review the progress-monitoring data.
- Plan and hold team learning celebration. Celebrate the things you value for students and staff.
- Plan and hold leadership team meeting.
- Determine learning focus of the staff meeting aligned with the district leadership team meeting and the building leadership team meeting held last month, and the school-improvement plan.
- Analyze data from next end-of-unit assessment and schedule vertical articulation team meetings based on data.
- Plan and hold MTSS/RTI and PBIS meeting.
- Report data to the school board.
- Plan for schoolwide social-emotional learning focus.

NOTES

November Management Work

- ☐ Hold staff meeting.
- ☐ Hold PTA or PTO meeting.
- ☐ Review emergency procedures and hold drills.
- ☐ Conduct midyear evaluation and growth goals check-ins with staff.

November Building Work

- ☐
- ☐
- ☐
- ☐
- ☐
- ☐
- ☐
- ☐

NOTES

NOVEMBER

Sunday	Monday	Tuesday	Wednesday	Thursday	Friday	Saturday

November

NOTES

DATE _____

November

MONDAY

TUESDAY

WEDNESDAY

THURSDAY

FRIDAY

COMPLETE TASK LIST

☐
☐
☐
☐
☐
☐
☐
☐
☐
☐
☐
☐
☐
☐
☐

NOTES

_____
_____
_____
_____
_____
_____
_____
_____

MUST-DO LIST

TEN-MINUTE TASKS

Phone Calls

Emails

Classrooms Check-Ins

Feedback and Follow-Up

Celebrations of Success

Positive Note

Positive Parent Connections

Self-Care Plan

Big Projects Ongoing or Upcoming

DATE _____

MONDAY

TUESDAY

WEDNESDAY

THURSDAY

FRIDAY

COMPLETE TASK LIST

- [ ]
- [ ]
- [ ]
- [ ]
- [ ]
- [ ]
- [ ]
- [ ]
- [ ]
- [ ]
- [ ]
- [ ]
- [ ]
- [ ]
- [ ]

NOTES

MUST-DO LIST

TEN-MINUTE TASKS

Phone Calls

Emails

Classrooms Check-Ins

Feedback and Follow-Up

Celebrations of Success

Positive Note

Positive Parent Connections

Self-Care Plan

Big Projects Ongoing or Upcoming

DATE _____

MONDAY

TUESDAY

November

WEDNESDAY

THURSDAY

FRIDAY

COMPLETE TASK LIST

☐
☐
☐
☐
☐
☐
☐
☐
☐
☐
☐
☐
☐
☐
☐
☐

NOTES

_____
_____
_____
_____
_____
_____
_____
_____
_____

MUST-DO LIST

TEN-MINUTE TASKS

Phone Calls

Emails

Classrooms Check-Ins

Feedback and Follow-Up

Celebrations of Success

Positive Note

Positive Parent Connections

Self-Care Plan

Big Projects Ongoing or Upcoming

DATE _____

MONDAY

TUESDAY

WEDNESDAY

THURSDAY

FRIDAY

COMPLETE TASK LIST

- [ ]
- [ ]
- [ ]
- [ ]
- [ ]
- [ ]
- [ ]
- [ ]
- [ ]
- [ ]
- [ ]
- [ ]
- [ ]
- [ ]
- [ ]

NOTES

_____
_____
_____
_____
_____
_____
_____
_____
_____

MUST-DO LIST

TEN-MINUTE TASKS

Phone Calls

Emails

Classrooms Check-Ins

Feedback and Follow-Up

Celebrations of Success

Positive Note

Positive Parent Connections

Self-Care Plan

Big Projects Ongoing or Upcoming

DATE _____

MONDAY

TUESDAY

WEDNESDAY

THURSDAY

FRIDAY

COMPLETE TASK LIST

☐
☐
☐
☐
☐
☐
☐
☐
☐
☐
☐
☐
☐
☐
☐
☐

NOTES

MUST-DO LIST

TEN-MINUTE TASKS

Phone Calls

Emails

Classrooms Check-Ins

Feedback and Follow-Up

Celebrations of Success

Positive Note

Positive Parent Connections

Self-Care Plan

Big Projects Ongoing or Upcoming

MY MONTHLY REFLECTIONS

November

ACCOMPLISHMENTS

WHAT WENT WELL

LESSONS LEARNED

WHAT TO CHANGE

Are there systems I can put in place that would make this month go smoother next year?

What is something I can simplify or do away with to improve this month next year?

DISTRICT LEADERSHIP MEETING COMMITMENTS

Use this tool to document commitments you or your building leadership team are making based on the work at this month's district leadership meeting.

Building leadership team meeting: _____ **Date:** _____

Commitments based on principal or building leadership team work:

Plan for next steps or work for building leadership team meeting:

Evidence of commitments:

DECEMBER

"

Frequent public acknowledgments for a job well done and a wide distribution of small symbolic gestures of appreciation and admiration are far more powerful tools for communicating priorities than infrequent "grand prizes" that create a few winners and many losers.

—Richard DuFour, Rebecca DuFour, Robert Eaker, and Thomas Many

DECEMBER PLC WORK

- Ensure the teacher observation schedule aligns with essential standards in content areas and grade levels.
- Visit collaborative meetings to observe evidence of the following.
  - Norms, accountability protocols, and collective commitments
  - Essential standards and learning targets
  - Data or student work at the team table
  - Discussion surrounding where students did well and instructional strategies that helped students
  - Discussion surrounding additional time, support, and extensions
  - Discussion surrounding the next targets and instructional strategies and formative assessment
- Review products from weekly collaborative meeting with administrative team, instructional coaches, and teachers on special assignment.
- Observe core instruction (Tier 1).
- Observe Tier 2 intervention. Is there a direct connection to core instruction?
- Observe Tier 3 intervention. What universal skills are being taught using a research-based curriculum? Review the progress-monitoring data.
- Plan and hold team learning celebration. Celebrate the things you value for students and staff.
- Plan and hold district leadership team meeting.
- Determine learning focus of the staff meeting aligned with the district leadership team meeting and the building leadership team meeting held last month, and the school-improvement plan.
- Analyze data from next end-of-unit assessment and schedule vertical articulation team meetings based on data.
- Plan and hold MTSS/RTI and PBIS meeting.
- Present data report to the board.
- Plan for schoolwide social-emotional learning focus.

NOTES

December Management Work

- ☐ Hold staff meeting.
- ☐ Hold PTA or PTO meeting.
- ☐ Review emergency procedures and hold drills.
- ☐ Conduct midyear evaluation and growth goals check-ins with staff.

December Building Work

- ☐
- ☐
- ☐
- ☐
- ☐
- ☐
- ☐
- ☐

NOTES

DECEMBER

Sunday	Monday	Tuesday	Wednesday	Thursday	Friday	Saturday

NOTES

DATE _____

MONDAY

TUESDAY

WEDNESDAY

THURSDAY

FRIDAY

COMPLETE TASK LIST

☐
☐
☐
☐
☐
☐
☐
☐
☐
☐
☐
☐
☐
☐
☐

NOTES

_____
_____
_____
_____
_____
_____
_____
_____
_____

MUST-DO LIST

TEN-MINUTE TASKS

Phone Calls

Emails

Classrooms Check-Ins

Feedback and Follow-Up

Celebrations of Success

Positive Note

Positive Parent Connections

Self-Care Plan

Big Projects Ongoing or Upcoming

DATE _____

MONDAY

TUESDAY

WEDNESDAY

THURSDAY

FRIDAY

COMPLETE TASK LIST

☐
☐
☐
☐
☐
☐
☐
☐
☐
☐
☐
☐
☐
☐
☐
☐
☐

NOTES

MUST-DO LIST

TEN-MINUTE TASKS

Phone Calls

Emails

Classrooms Check-Ins

Feedback and Follow-Up

Celebrations of Success

Positive Note

Positive Parent Connections

Self-Care Plan

Big Projects Ongoing or Upcoming

DATE _____

December

MONDAY

TUESDAY

WEDNESDAY

THURSDAY

FRIDAY

COMPLETE TASK LIST

☐
☐
☐
☐
☐
☐
☐
☐
☐
☐
☐
☐
☐
☐
☐

NOTES

_____
_____
_____
_____
_____
_____
_____
_____

MUST-DO LIST

TEN-MINUTE TASKS

Phone Calls

Emails

Classrooms Check-Ins

Feedback and Follow-Up

Celebrations of Success

Positive Note

Positive Parent Connections

Self-Care Plan

Big Projects Ongoing or Upcoming

DATE _____

MONDAY

TUESDAY

WEDNESDAY

THURSDAY

FRIDAY

COMPLETE TASK LIST

☐
☐
☐
☐
☐
☐
☐
☐
☐
☐
☐
☐
☐
☐
☐

NOTES

MUST-DO LIST

TEN-MINUTE TASKS

Phone Calls

Emails

Classrooms Check-Ins

Feedback and Follow-Up

Celebrations of Success

Positive Note

Positive Parent Connections

Self-Care Plan

Big Projects Ongoing or Upcoming

DATE _____

MONDAY

TUESDAY

WEDNESDAY

THURSDAY

FRIDAY

COMPLETE TASK LIST

☐
☐
☐
☐
☐
☐
☐
☐
☐
☐
☐
☐
☐
☐
☐
☐

NOTES

_____
_____
_____
_____
_____
_____
_____
_____
_____

MUST-DO LIST

TEN-MINUTE TASKS

Phone Calls

Emails

Classrooms Check-Ins

Feedback and Follow-Up

Celebrations of Success

Positive Note

Positive Parent Connections

Self-Care Plan

Big Projects Ongoing or Upcoming

MY MONTHLY REFLECTIONS

December

ACCOMPLISHMENTS

WHAT WENT WELL

LESSONS LEARNED

WHAT TO CHANGE

Are there systems I can put in place that would make this month go smoother next year?

What is something I can simplify or do away with to improve this month next year?

DISTRICT LEADERSHIP MEETING COMMITMENTS

Use this tool to document commitments you or your building leadership team are making based on the work at this month's district leadership meeting.

Building leadership team meeting: _____ **Date:** _____

Commitments based on principal or building leadership team work:

Plan for next steps or work for building leadership team meeting:

Evidence of commitments:

Midyear Reflection

> Working hard for something we do not care about is called stress; working hard for something we love is called passion.
>
> —Simon Sinek

When Richard DuFour was principal of Adlai E. Stevenson High School, he was known for making decisions easily. Rick would often say, "When you know your *why*, your *what* has more impact because you are walking in and toward your purpose" (T. Kanold, personal communication, September 1, 2019). In other words, when you know why you have a goal, making decisions becomes very easy—if the decision doesn't support your reasons for pursuing the goal, the answer is *no*.

As these planning pages show, educational leaders start their planning for the new year halfway through the current school year. This can be exhausting and stressful. It helps to reflect and refocus and get back to the *why* to reignite passion for the work. As you come back from winter break, it's time to focus specifically on students who are still not meeting standards. Ask, "Is our core instruction solid?" All students can learn if we establish high standards. Reflect on the interventions being used in Tiers 2 and 3. Are they working? If not, what is the plan? What changes need to be made so that *every* student is successful? Now is not the time to lose focus.

What were your big goals at the start of the school year? Are you continuing to be proactive and consistent as you work toward them? Are you engaging in small, daily actions that are focused on achieving your goals? How can you ensure that you meet, or even surpass, the goals you set? Gail Matthews (2015), a psychology professor at Dominican University of California, did a study on goal setting that examined the behaviors of a diverse group of 267 people. The results of the study (Matthews, 2015) suggest that those who write down their goals and dreams on a regular basis achieve what they want at a much higher rate than those who do not. As a result, Matthews (2015) finds that you become 42 percent more likely to accomplish your goals simply by writing them down regularly.

The "Setting Professional and Personal Goals" reproducible and the "Goal-Setting Worksheet" reproducible in part 3 (pages 219 and 220) will help you set goals and achieve them.

Long-term goal setting is very important, but also consider, what can you *do now* with a sense of purpose? As our year goes on, we can easily become mired in the minutia of daily tasks and lose sight of our direction and goals. It's easy to put off things that don't have deadlines, like staff celebrations. What is your plan for finishing the school year strong?

Eudaemonia (n.d.) means "human flourishing"; it is "a contented state of being happy and healthy and prosperous." Take care of yourself and your staff to make achieving such fulfillment a reality. We can't *give* if we aren't *full*. Planning is action and action in the service of education *is* giving, giving of effort, thought, and time. We cannot give if we are running on empty ourselves. Make sure you set strong goals around this as well.

JANUARY

> "
>
> The question confronting most schools and districts is not, "What do we need to know in order to improve?" but rather, "Will we turn what we already know into action?"
>
> **—Richard DuFour, Rebecca DuFour, Robert Eaker, Thomas Many, and Mike Mattos**

JANUARY PLC WORK

- Ensure teacher observation schedule aligns with essential standards in content areas and grade levels.
- Visit collaborative meetings to observe evidence of the following.
  - Norms, accountability protocols, and collective commitments
  - Essential standards and learning targets
  - Data or student work at the team table
  - Discussion surrounding where students did well and instructional strategies that helped students
  - Discussion surrounding additional time, support, and extensions
  - Discussion surrounding the next targets and instructional strategies and formative assessment
- Review products from weekly collaborative meeting with administrative team, instructional coaches, and teachers on special assignment.
- Review benchmark assessment results and progress-monitoring data.
- Review end-of-semester grades.
- Analyze data from next end-of-unit assessment and schedule vertical articulation team meetings based on the data.
- Present data to the district team to include the results of:
  - Fall and winter benchmark assessments
  - Unit assessments
  - Attendance data
  - Discipline data
  - Subgroup and historically under-represented student data
- Observe core instruction (Tier 1).
- Observe Tier 2 intervention. Is there a direct connection to core instruction?
- Observe Tier 3 intervention. What universal skills are being taught using a research-based curriculum? Review the progress-monitoring data.
- Plan and hold leadership team meeting.
- Plan and hold team learning celebration. Celebrate the things you value for students and staff.
- Determine learning focus of the staff meeting aligned the district leadership team meeting and the building leadership team meeting held last month, and the school-improvement plan.
- Plan and hold MTSS/RTI and PBIS meeting.
- Present data report to the board.
- Plan for schoolwide social-emotional learning focus.

NOTES

January Management Work

- ☐ Revisit PBIS expectations.
- ☐ Hold staff meeting.
- ☐ Hold PTA or PTO meeting.
- ☐ Review emergency procedures and hold drills.
- ☐ Conduct benchmark testing.
- ☐ Communicate finals plan.
- ☐ Distribute report cards.

January Building Work

- ☐
- ☐
- ☐
- ☐
- ☐
- ☐
- ☐
- ☐

January

NOTES

JANUARY

Sunday	Monday	Tuesday	Wednesday	Thursday	Friday	Saturday

January

NOTES

January

DATE _____

MONDAY

TUESDAY

WEDNESDAY

THURSDAY

FRIDAY

COMPLETE TASK LIST

☐
☐
☐
☐
☐
☐
☐
☐
☐
☐
☐
☐
☐
☐
☐
☐

NOTES

MUST-DO LIST

TEN-MINUTE TASKS

Phone Calls

Emails

Classrooms Check-Ins

Feedback and Follow-Up

Celebrations of Success

Positive Note

Positive Parent Connections

Self-Care Plan

Big Projects Ongoing or Upcoming

DATE _____

MONDAY

TUESDAY

WEDNESDAY

THURSDAY

FRIDAY

COMPLETE TASK LIST

- [ ]
- [ ]
- [ ]
- [ ]
- [ ]
- [ ]
- [ ]
- [ ]
- [ ]
- [ ]
- [ ]
- [ ]
- [ ]
- [ ]
- [ ]

NOTES

_____
_____
_____
_____
_____
_____
_____
_____

MUST-DO LIST

TEN-MINUTE TASKS

Phone Calls

Emails

Classrooms Check-Ins

Feedback and Follow-Up

Celebrations of Success

Positive Note

Positive Parent Connections

Self-Care Plan

Big Projects Ongoing or Upcoming

DATE _____

MONDAY

TUESDAY

WEDNESDAY

THURSDAY

FRIDAY

COMPLETE TASK LIST

☐
☐
☐
☐
☐
☐
☐
☐
☐
☐
☐
☐
☐
☐
☐

NOTES

MUST-DO LIST

TEN-MINUTE TASKS

Phone Calls

Emails

Classrooms Check-Ins

Feedback and Follow-Up

Celebrations of Success

Positive Note

Positive Parent Connections

Self-Care Plan

Big Projects Ongoing or Upcoming

DATE _____

MONDAY

TUESDAY

WEDNESDAY

THURSDAY

FRIDAY

COMPLETE TASK LIST

☐
☐
☐
☐
☐
☐
☐
☐
☐
☐
☐
☐
☐
☐
☐

NOTES

MUST-DO LIST

TEN-MINUTE TASKS

Phone Calls

Emails

Classrooms Check-Ins

Feedback and Follow-Up

Celebrations of Success

Positive Note

Positive Parent Connections

Self-Care Plan

Big Projects Ongoing or Upcoming

DATE _____

MONDAY

TUESDAY

WEDNESDAY

THURSDAY

FRIDAY

COMPLETE TASK LIST

- ☐
- ☐
- ☐
- ☐
- ☐
- ☐
- ☐
- ☐
- ☐
- ☐
- ☐
- ☐
- ☐
- ☐
- ☐
- ☐

NOTES

_____
_____
_____
_____
_____
_____
_____
_____
_____

MUST-DO LIST

TEN-MINUTE TASKS

Phone Calls

Emails

Classrooms Check-Ins

Feedback and Follow-Up

Celebrations of Success

Positive Note

Positive Parent Connections

Self-Care Plan

Big Projects Ongoing or Upcoming

MY MONTHLY REFLECTIONS

ACCOMPLISHMENTS

WHAT WENT WELL

LESSONS LEARNED

WHAT TO CHANGE

Are there systems I can put in place that would make this month go smoother next year?

What is something I can simplify or do away with to improve this month next year?

DISTRICT LEADERSHIP MEETING COMMITMENTS

Use this tool to document commitments you or your building leadership team are making based on the work at this month's district leadership meeting.

Building leadership team meeting: _____ **Date:** _____

Commitments based on principal or building leadership team work:

Plan for next steps or work for building leadership team meeting:

Evidence of commitments:

FEBRUARY

> **"**
>
> Here is the brutal fact: The most common reason for failure to close the knowing-doing gap is not conflict with others, but conflict from within. We fail to do what we recognize we should do simply because it is easier to continue an unquestionably ineffective or bad practice than it is to adopt a new one.
>
> **—Richard DuFour, Rebecca DuFour, Robert Eaker, and Thomas Many**

FEBRUARY PLC WORK

- Ensure teacher observation schedule aligns with essential standards in content areas and grade levels.
- Visit collaborative meetings to observe evidence of the following.
  - Norms, accountability protocols, and collective commitments
  - Essential standards and learning targets
  - Data or student work at the team table
  - Discussion surrounding where students did well and instructional strategies that helped students
  - Discussion surrounding additional time, support, and extensions
  - Discussion surrounding the next targets and instructional strategies and formative assessment
- Review products from weekly collaborative meeting with administrative team, instructional coaches, and teachers on special assignment.
- Observe core instruction (Tier 1).
- Observe Tier 2 intervention. Is there a direct connection to core instruction?
- Observe Tier 3 intervention. What universal skills are being taught using a research-based curriculum? Review the progress-monitoring data.
- Plan team learning celebration. Celebrate the things you value for students and staff.
- Plan and hold leadership team meeting.
- Determine learning focus of the staff meeting aligned with the district leadership team meeting and the building leadership team meeting held last month, and the school-improvement plan.
- Analyze data from next end-of-unit assessment and schedule vertical articulation team meetings based on data.
- Plan and hold MTSS/RTI and PBIS meeting.
- Provide data report to the school board.
- Plan for schoolwide social-emotional learning focus.

NOTES

February Management Work

- ☐ Hold staff meeting.
- ☐ Hold PTA or PTO meeting.
- ☐ Review emergency procedures and hold drills.

February Building Work

- ☐
- ☐
- ☐
- ☐
- ☐
- ☐
- ☐
- ☐

NOTES

February

FEBRUARY						
Sunday	Monday	Tuesday	Wednesday	Thursday	Friday	Saturday

NOTES

DATE _____

MONDAY

TUESDAY

WEDNESDAY

THURSDAY

FRIDAY

COMPLETE TASK LIST

- [ ]
- [ ]
- [ ]
- [ ]
- [ ]
- [ ]
- [ ]
- [ ]
- [ ]
- [ ]
- [ ]
- [ ]
- [ ]
- [ ]
- [ ]

NOTES

MUST-DO LIST

TEN-MINUTE TASKS

Phone Calls

Emails

Classrooms Check-Ins

Feedback and Follow-Up

Celebrations of Success

Positive Note

Positive Parent Connections

Self-Care Plan

Big Projects Ongoing or Upcoming

DATE _____

MONDAY

TUESDAY

WEDNESDAY

THURSDAY

FRIDAY

COMPLETE TASK LIST

- [ ]
- [ ]
- [ ]
- [ ]
- [ ]
- [ ]
- [ ]
- [ ]
- [ ]
- [ ]
- [ ]
- [ ]
- [ ]
- [ ]
- [ ]

NOTES

_____
_____
_____
_____
_____
_____
_____
_____
_____

MUST-DO LIST

TEN-MINUTE TASKS

Phone Calls

Emails

Classrooms Check-Ins

Feedback and Follow-Up

Celebrations of Success

Positive Note

Positive Parent Connections

Self-Care Plan

Big Projects Ongoing or Upcoming

DATE _____

MONDAY

TUESDAY

WEDNESDAY

THURSDAY

FRIDAY

COMPLETE TASK LIST

☐
☐
☐
☐
☐
☐
☐
☐
☐
☐
☐
☐
☐
☐
☐
☐

NOTES

MUST-DO LIST

TEN-MINUTE TASKS

Phone Calls

Emails

Classrooms Check-Ins

Feedback and Follow-Up

Celebrations of Success

Positive Note

Positive Parent Connections

Self-Care Plan

Big Projects Ongoing or Upcoming

DATE _____

MONDAY

TUESDAY

WEDNESDAY

THURSDAY

FRIDAY

COMPLETE TASK LIST

☐
☐
☐
☐
☐
☐
☐
☐
☐
☐
☐
☐
☐
☐
☐

NOTES
_____
_____
_____
_____
_____
_____
_____
_____
_____

MUST-DO LIST

TEN-MINUTE TASKS

Phone Calls

Emails

Classrooms Check-Ins

Feedback and Follow-Up

Celebrations of Success

Positive Note

Positive Parent Connections

Self-Care Plan

Big Projects Ongoing or Upcoming

February

DATE _____

MONDAY

TUESDAY

WEDNESDAY

THURSDAY

FRIDAY

COMPLETE TASK LIST

☐
☐
☐
☐
☐
☐
☐
☐
☐
☐
☐
☐
☐
☐
☐
☐

NOTES

_____
_____
_____
_____
_____
_____
_____
_____
_____

February

MUST-DO LIST

TEN-MINUTE TASKS

Phone Calls

Emails

Classrooms Check-Ins

Feedback and Follow-Up

Celebrations of Success

Positive Note

Positive Parent Connections

Self-Care Plan

Big Projects Ongoing or Upcoming

MY MONTHLY REFLECTIONS

ACCOMPLISHMENTS

WHAT WENT WELL

LESSONS LEARNED

WHAT TO CHANGE

Are there systems I can put in place that would make this month go smoother next year?

What is something I can simplify or do away with to improve this month next year?

DISTRICT LEADERSHIP MEETING COMMITMENTS

Use this tool to document commitments you or your building leadership team are making based on the work at this month's district leadership meeting.

Building leadership team meeting: _____ **Date:** _____

Commitments based on principal or building leadership team work:

Plan for next steps or work for building leadership team meeting:

Evidence of commitments:

MARCH

> "
>
> Isn't it ironic how
> frequently we question
> the willingness of others
> to do what must be
> done to improve our
> schools, and in doing
> so, we absolve ourselves
> of the responsibility for
> taking action?
>
> **—Robert Eaker, Richard
> DuFour, and Rebecca DuFour**

MARCH PLC WORK

- Ensure teacher observation schedule aligns with essential standards in content areas and grade levels.
- Visit collaborative meetings to observe evidence of the following.
  - Norms, accountability protocols, and collective commitments
  - Essential standards and learning targets
  - Data or student work at the team table
  - Discussion surrounding where students did well and instructional strategies that helped students
  - Discussion surrounding additional time, support, and extensions
  - Discussion surrounding the next targets and instructional strategies and formative assessment
- Review products from weekly collaborative meeting with administrative team, instructional coaches, and teachers on special assignment.
- Analyze data from next end-of-unit assessment and schedule vertical articulation team meetings based on data.
- Observe core instruction (Tier 1).
- Observe Tier 2 intervention. Is there a direct connection to core instruction?
- Observe Tier 3 intervention. What universal skills are being taught using a research-based curriculum? Review the progress-monitoring data.
- Plan and hold leadership team meeting.
- Plan team learning celebration. Celebrate the things you value for students and staff.
- Determine learning focus of the staff meeting aligned with the district leadership team meeting and the building leadership team meeting held last month, and the school-improvement plan.
- Plan and hold MTSS/RTI and PBIS meeting.
- Present data report to the board.
- Design master schedule for the next school year. Does it reflect what you value?
  - Collaboration time
  - Additional time, support, and extensions (Tiers 2 and 3)
  - Uninterrupted blocks of time for core instruction
- Ensure the hiring process includes questions surrounding collaboration.
- Ensure all new hires understand what it means to work in a school that is a PLC at Work before offering them a contract.
- Review data to make decisions about cotaught classes.
- Review course requests to plan for singleton courses.
- Review data and grades to plan for students needing to repeat required courses.
- Plan professional development for any approved new courses.
- Review staffing needs based on enrollment and team dynamics.
- Plan for schoolwide social-emotional learning focus.

March Management Work

- [ ] Hold staff meeting.
- [ ] Hold PTA or PTO meeting.
- [ ] Review emergency procedures and hold drills.
- [ ] Mark calendar for upcoming job and recruiting events, decide who will attend, and work with human resources on potential job openings.
- [ ] Conduct parent, teacher, and student conferences.
- [ ] Hold celebration for Classified Employee Appreciation Week.
- [ ] Meet with assessment coordinator to plan for state assessment.
- [ ] Plan for AP and IB testing (secondary level).

March Building Work

- [ ]
- [ ]
- [ ]
- [ ]
- [ ]
- [ ]
- [ ]
- [ ]

NOTES

MARCH

Sunday	Monday	Tuesday	Wednesday	Thursday	Friday	Saturday

NOTES

DATE _____

MONDAY

TUESDAY

WEDNESDAY

THURSDAY

FRIDAY

COMPLETE TASK LIST

- [ ]
- [ ]
- [ ]
- [ ]
- [ ]
- [ ]
- [ ]
- [ ]
- [ ]
- [ ]
- [ ]
- [ ]
- [ ]
- [ ]
- [ ]

NOTES

_____
_____
_____
_____
_____
_____
_____
_____

MUST-DO LIST

TEN-MINUTE TASKS

Phone Calls

Emails

Classrooms Check-Ins

Feedback and Follow-Up

Celebrations of Success

Positive Note

Positive Parent Connections

Self-Care Plan

Big Projects Ongoing or Upcoming

DATE _____

MONDAY

TUESDAY

WEDNESDAY

THURSDAY

FRIDAY

COMPLETE TASK LIST

☐
☐
☐
☐
☐
☐
☐
☐
☐
☐
☐
☐
☐
☐
☐
☐

NOTES

_____
_____
_____
_____
_____
_____
_____
_____
_____

March

MUST-DO LIST

TEN-MINUTE TASKS

Phone Calls

Emails

Classrooms Check-Ins

Feedback and Follow-Up

Celebrations of Success

Positive Note

Positive Parent Connections

Self-Care Plan

Big Projects Ongoing or Upcoming

DATE _____

MONDAY

TUESDAY

WEDNESDAY

THURSDAY

FRIDAY

COMPLETE TASK LIST

☐
☐
☐
☐
☐
☐
☐
☐
☐
☐
☐
☐
☐
☐
☐

NOTES

_____
_____
_____
_____
_____
_____
_____
_____
_____

MUST-DO LIST

TEN-MINUTE TASKS

Phone Calls

Emails

Classrooms Check-Ins

Feedback and Follow-Up

Celebrations of Success

Positive Note

Positive Parent Connections

Self-Care Plan

Big Projects Ongoing or Upcoming

DATE _____

MONDAY

TUESDAY

WEDNESDAY

THURSDAY

FRIDAY

COMPLETE TASK LIST

☐
☐
☐
☐
☐
☐
☐
☐
☐
☐
☐
☐
☐
☐
☐

NOTES

_____
_____
_____
_____
_____
_____
_____
_____
_____

March

MUST-DO LIST

TEN-MINUTE TASKS

Phone Calls

Emails

Classrooms Check-Ins

Feedback and Follow-Up

Celebrations of Success

Positive Note

Positive Parent Connections

Self-Care Plan

Big Projects Ongoing or Upcoming

DATE _____

MONDAY

TUESDAY

WEDNESDAY

THURSDAY

FRIDAY

COMPLETE TASK LIST

☐
☐
☐
☐
☐
☐
☐
☐
☐
☐
☐
☐
☐
☐
☐

NOTES

_____
_____
_____
_____
_____
_____
_____
_____
_____

MUST-DO LIST

TEN-MINUTE TASKS

Phone Calls

Emails

Classrooms Check-Ins

Feedback and Follow-Up

Celebrations of Success

Positive Note

Positive Parent Connections

Self-Care Plan

Big Projects Ongoing or Upcoming

MY MONTHLY REFLECTIONS

ACCOMPLISHMENTS

WHAT WENT WELL

LESSONS LEARNED

WHAT TO CHANGE

Are there systems I can put in place that would make this month go smoother next year?

What is something I can simplify or do away with to improve this month next year?

March

DISTRICT LEADERSHIP MEETING COMMITMENTS

Use this tool to document commitments you or your building leadership team are making based on the work at this month's district leadership meeting.

Building leadership team meeting: _____ **Date:** _____

Commitments based on principal or building leadership team work:

Plan for next steps or work for building leadership team meeting:

Evidence of commitments:

APRIL

> **"**
>
> Any assessment
> process must begin
> by defining what it
> means to succeed.
>
> **—Richard DuFour and
> Robert Eaker**

APRIL PLC WORK

- Visit collaborative meetings to observe evidence of the following.
  - Norms, accountability protocols, and collective commitments
  - Essential standards and learning targets
  - Data or student work at the team table
  - Discussion surrounding where students did well and instructional strategies that helped students
  - Discussion surrounding additional time, support, and extensions
  - Discussion surrounding the next targets and instructional strategies and formative assessment
- Review products from weekly collaborative meeting with administrative team, instructional coaches, and teachers on special assignment.
- Present data to the district leadership team including the results of fall and winter benchmark assessments, unit assessments, attendance data, discipline data, and subgroup data.
- Observe core instruction (Tier 1).
- Observe Tier 2 intervention. Is there a direct connection to core instruction?
- Observe Tier 3 intervention. What universal skills are being taught using a research-based curriculum? Review the progress-monitoring data.
- Plan team learning celebration. Celebrate the things you value for students and staff.
- Plan and hold leadership team meeting.
- Determine learning focus of the staff meeting aligned with the district leadership team meeting and the building leadership team meeting held last month, and the school-improvement plan.
- Analyze data from next end-of-unit assessment and schedule vertical articulation team meetings based on data.
- Plan and hold MTSS/RTI and PBIS meeting.
- Craft evaluations that highlight student growth and evidence of the work of teacher teams.
- Present data report to the board.
- Plan for schoolwide social-emotional learning focus.
- Ensure the hiring process includes questions surrounding collaboration.
- Ensure all new hires understand what it means to work in a school that is a PLC at Work before offering them a contract.

NOTES

April Management Work

- [ ] Hold staff meeting.
- [ ] Hold PTA or PTO meeting.
- [ ] Review emergency procedures and hold drills.
- [ ] Hire staff.
- [ ] Conduct parent, teacher, and student conferences
- [ ] Conduct state assessment.

April Building Work

- [ ]
- [ ]
- [ ]
- [ ]
- [ ]
- [ ]
- [ ]
- [ ]

NOTES

April

APRIL						
Sunday	Monday	Tuesday	Wednesday	Thursday	Friday	Saturday

NOTES

DATE _____

MONDAY

TUESDAY

WEDNESDAY

THURSDAY

FRIDAY

COMPLETE TASK LIST

☐
☐
☐
☐
☐
☐
☐
☐
☐
☐
☐
☐
☐
☐
☐

NOTES

_____
_____
_____
_____
_____
_____
_____
_____
_____

April

MUST-DO LIST

TEN-MINUTE TASKS

Phone Calls

Emails

Classrooms Check-Ins

Feedback and Follow-Up

Celebrations of Success

Positive Note

Positive Parent Connections

Self-Care Plan

Big Projects Ongoing or Upcoming

DATE _____

MONDAY

TUESDAY

WEDNESDAY

THURSDAY

FRIDAY

COMPLETE TASK LIST

- [ ]
- [ ]
- [ ]
- [ ]
- [ ]
- [ ]
- [ ]
- [ ]
- [ ]
- [ ]
- [ ]
- [ ]
- [ ]
- [ ]
- [ ]

NOTES

_____
_____
_____
_____
_____
_____
_____
_____

April

MUST-DO LIST

TEN-MINUTE TASKS

Phone Calls

Emails

Classrooms Check-Ins

Feedback and Follow-Up

Celebrations of Success

Positive Note

Positive Parent Connections

Self-Care Plan

Big Projects Ongoing or Upcoming

April

DATE _____

MONDAY

TUESDAY

WEDNESDAY

THURSDAY

FRIDAY

COMPLETE TASK LIST

☐
☐
☐
☐
☐
☐
☐
☐
☐
☐
☐
☐
☐
☐
☐

NOTES

April

MUST-DO LIST

TEN-MINUTE TASKS

Phone Calls

Emails

Classrooms Check-Ins

Feedback and Follow-Up

Celebrations of Success

Positive Note

Positive Parent Connections

Self-Care Plan

Big Projects Ongoing or Upcoming

DATE _____

MONDAY

TUESDAY

WEDNESDAY

THURSDAY

April

FRIDAY

COMPLETE TASK LIST

☐
☐
☐
☐
☐
☐
☐
☐
☐
☐
☐
☐
☐
☐
☐
☐

NOTES

_____
_____
_____
_____
_____
_____
_____
_____
_____

MUST-DO LIST

TEN-MINUTE TASKS

Phone Calls

Emails

Classrooms Check-Ins

Feedback and Follow-Up

Celebrations of Success

Positive Note

Positive Parent Connections

Self-Care Plan

Big Projects Ongoing or Upcoming

DATE _____

MONDAY

TUESDAY

WEDNESDAY

THURSDAY

April

FRIDAY

COMPLETE TASK LIST

☐
☐
☐
☐
☐
☐
☐
☐
☐
☐
☐
☐
☐
☐
☐

NOTES

_____
_____
_____
_____
_____
_____
_____
_____
_____

MUST-DO LIST

TEN-MINUTE TASKS

Phone Calls

Emails

Classrooms Check-Ins

Feedback and Follow-Up

Celebrations of Success

Positive Note

Positive Parent Connections

Self-Care Plan

Big Projects Ongoing or Upcoming

MY MONTHLY REFLECTIONS

ACCOMPLISHMENTS

WHAT WENT WELL

LESSONS LEARNED

WHAT TO CHANGE

Are there systems I can put in place that would make this month go smoother next year?

What is something I can simplify or do away with to improve this month next year?

April

DISTRICT LEADERSHIP MEETING COMMITMENTS

Use this tool to document commitments you or your building leadership team are making based on the work at this month's district leadership meeting.

Building leadership team meeting: _____ **Date:** _____

Commitments based on principal or building leadership team work:

Plan for next steps or work for building leadership team meeting:

Evidence of commitments:

MAY

> **"**
>
> If schools are to
> improve, they
> need educators
> who believe in the
> possibility of a better
> future—and in
> themselves.
>
> **—Richard DuFour and
> Robert Eaker**

MAY PLC WORK

- Visit collaborative meetings to observe evidence of the following.
  - Norms, accountability protocols, and collective commitments
  - Essential standards and learning targets
  - Data or student work at the team table
  - Discussion surrounding where students did well and instructional strategies that helped students
  - Discussion surrounding additional time, support, and extensions
  - Discussion surrounding the next targets and instructional strategies and formative assessment
- Review products from weekly collaborative meeting with administrative team, instructional coaches, and teachers on special assignment.
- Observe core instruction (Tier 1).
- Observe Tier 2 intervention. Is there a direct connection to core instruction?
- Observe Tier 3 intervention. What universal skills are being taught using a research-based curriculum? Review the progress-monitoring data.
- Plan team learning celebration. Celebrate the things you value for students and staff.
- Plan and hold leadership team meeting.
- Determine learning focus of the staff meeting aligned with the district leadership team meeting and the building leadership team meeting held last month, and the school-improvement plan.
- Analyze data from next end-of-unit assessment.
- Plan and hold MTSS/RTI and PBIS meeting.
- Present data report to the board.
- Plan for schoolwide social-emotional learning focus.
- Establish teams for the next school year (including making new hires and grade-level and content-area changes).
- Ensure the hiring process includes questions surrounding collaboration.
- Ensure all new hires understand what it means to work in a school that is a PLC at Work before offering them a contract.

NOTES

May Management Work

- ☐ Hold staff meeting.
- ☐ Hold PTA or PTO meeting.
- ☐ Review emergency procedures and hold drills.
- ☐ Hire staff.
- ☐ Conduct parent, teacher, and student conferences.
- ☐ Plan for Teacher Appreciation Week.
- ☐ Evaluate certificated and classified staff.
- ☐ Make staffing assignments for next year.
- ☐ Conduct state assessment.
- ☐ Conduct AP testing.

May Building Work

- ☐
- ☐
- ☐
- ☐
- ☐
- ☐
- ☐
- ☐

NOTES

MAY

Sunday	Monday	Tuesday	Wednesday	Thursday	Friday	Saturday

NOTES

DATE _____

MONDAY

TUESDAY

WEDNESDAY

THURSDAY

FRIDAY

COMPLETE TASK LIST

☐
☐
☐
☐
☐
☐
☐
☐
☐
☐
☐
☐
☐
☐
☐

NOTES

_____
_____
_____
_____
_____
_____
_____
_____
_____

MUST-DO LIST

TEN-MINUTE TASKS

Phone Calls

Emails

Classrooms Check-Ins

Feedback and Follow-Up

Celebrations of Success

Positive Note

Positive Parent Connections

Self-Care Plan

Big Projects Ongoing or Upcoming

DATE _____

MONDAY

TUESDAY

WEDNESDAY

THURSDAY

FRIDAY

COMPLETE TASK LIST

☐
☐
☐
☐
☐
☐
☐
☐
☐
☐
☐
☐
☐
☐
☐

NOTES

_____
_____
_____
_____
_____
_____
_____
_____

May

MUST-DO LIST

TEN-MINUTE TASKS

Phone Calls

Emails

Classrooms Check-Ins

Feedback and Follow-Up

Celebrations of Success

Positive Note

Positive Parent Connections

Self-Care Plan

May

Big Projects Ongoing or Upcoming

DATE _____

MONDAY

TUESDAY

WEDNESDAY

THURSDAY

FRIDAY

COMPLETE TASK LIST

- [ ]
- [ ]
- [ ]
- [ ]
- [ ]
- [ ]
- [ ]
- [ ]
- [ ]
- [ ]
- [ ]
- [ ]
- [ ]
- [ ]
- [ ]

NOTES

_____
_____
_____
_____
_____
_____
_____
_____
_____

May

MUST-DO LIST

TEN-MINUTE TASKS

Phone Calls

Emails

Classrooms Check-Ins

Feedback and Follow-Up

Celebrations of Success

Positive Note

Positive Parent Connections

Self-Care Plan

Big Projects Ongoing or Upcoming

May

DATE _____

MONDAY

TUESDAY

WEDNESDAY

THURSDAY

FRIDAY

COMPLETE TASK LIST

☐
☐
☐
☐
☐
☐
☐
☐
☐
☐
☐
☐
☐
☐
☐

NOTES

_____
_____
_____
_____
_____
_____
_____
_____

May

MUST-DO LIST

TEN-MINUTE TASKS

Phone Calls

Emails

Classrooms Check-Ins

Feedback and Follow-Up

Celebrations of Success

Positive Note

Positive Parent Connections

Self-Care Plan

Big Projects Ongoing or Upcoming

DATE _____

MONDAY

TUESDAY

WEDNESDAY

THURSDAY

FRIDAY

COMPLETE TASK LIST

☐
☐
☐
☐
☐
☐
☐
☐
☐
☐
☐
☐
☐
☐
☐

NOTES

_____
_____
_____
_____
_____
_____
_____
_____
_____

MUST-DO LIST

TEN-MINUTE TASKS

Phone Calls

Emails

Classrooms Check-Ins

Feedback and Follow-Up

Celebrations of Success

Positive Note

Positive Parent Connections

Self-Care Plan

Big Projects Ongoing or Upcoming

MY MONTHLY REFLECTIONS

ACCOMPLISHMENTS

WHAT WENT WELL

LESSONS LEARNED

WHAT TO CHANGE

Are there systems I can put in place that would make this month go smoother next year?

What is something I can simplify or do away with to improve this month next year?

May

DISTRICT LEADERSHIP MEETING COMMITMENTS

Use this tool to document commitments you or your building leadership team are making based on the work at this month's district leadership meeting.

Building leadership team meeting: _____ **Date:** _____

Commitments based on principal or building leadership team work:

Plan for next steps or work for building leadership team meeting:

Evidence of commitments:

JUNE

> "
>
> Professional learning
> communities set out to restore
> and increase the passion of
> teachers by not only reminding
> them of the moral purpose of
> their work, but also by creating
> the conditions that allow them to
> do that work successfully.
>
> **—Richard DuFour, Rebecca DuFour,
> Robert Eaker, and Thomas Many**

JUNE PLC WORK

- Review state assessment results.

- Review second-semester grades.

- Make data presentation to the district leadership team and celebrate the results of the following.

  - Fall, winter, and spring benchmark assessments

  - Unit assessments

  - State assessment

  - Attendance data

  - Discipline data

  - Subgroup data

  - Graduation rate (if applicable)

- Attend PLC conference or conduct PLC training activities in June, July, or August.

- Attend RTI conference or conduct RTI training activities.

NOTES

June Management Work

- [ ]
- [ ]
- [ ]
- [ ]
- [ ]
- [ ]
- [ ]
- [ ]

June Building Work

- [ ]
- [ ]
- [ ]
- [ ]
- [ ]
- [ ]
- [ ]
- [ ]

NOTES

JUNE

Sunday	Monday	Tuesday	Wednesday	Thursday	Friday	Saturday

NOTES

DATE _____

MONDAY

TUESDAY

WEDNESDAY

THURSDAY

FRIDAY

COMPLETE TASK LIST

☐
☐
☐
☐
☐
☐
☐
☐
☐
☐
☐
☐
☐
☐
☐

NOTES

MUST-DO LIST

TEN-MINUTE TASKS

Phone Calls

Emails

Classrooms Check-Ins

Feedback and Follow-Up

Celebrations of Success

Positive Note

Positive Parent Connections

Self-Care Plan

Big Projects Ongoing or Upcoming

June

DATE _____

MONDAY

TUESDAY

WEDNESDAY

THURSDAY

FRIDAY

COMPLETE TASK LIST

☐
☐
☐
☐
☐
☐
☐
☐
☐
☐
☐
☐
☐
☐
☐

NOTES

MUST-DO LIST

TEN-MINUTE TASKS

Phone Calls

Emails

Classrooms Check-Ins

Feedback and Follow-Up

Celebrations of Success

Positive Note

Positive Parent Connections

Self-Care Plan

Big Projects Ongoing or Upcoming

DATE _____

MONDAY

TUESDAY

WEDNESDAY

THURSDAY

FRIDAY

COMPLETE TASK LIST

☐
☐
☐
☐
☐
☐
☐
☐
☐
☐
☐
☐
☐
☐
☐

NOTES

_____
_____
_____
_____
_____
_____
_____
_____
_____

June

MUST-DO LIST

TEN-MINUTE TASKS

Phone Calls

Emails

Classrooms Check-Ins

Feedback and Follow-Up

Celebrations of Success

Positive Note

Positive Parent Connections

Self-Care Plan

Big Projects Ongoing or Upcoming

DATE _____

MONDAY

TUESDAY

WEDNESDAY

THURSDAY

FRIDAY

COMPLETE TASK LIST

- ☐
- ☐
- ☐
- ☐
- ☐
- ☐
- ☐
- ☐
- ☐
- ☐
- ☐
- ☐
- ☐
- ☐
- ☐

NOTES

_____
_____
_____
_____
_____
_____
_____
_____
_____
_____

MUST-DO LIST

TEN-MINUTE TASKS

Phone Calls

Emails

Classrooms Check-Ins

Feedback and Follow-Up

Celebrations of Success

Positive Note

Positive Parent Connections

Self-Care Plan

Big Projects Ongoing or Upcoming

June

DATE _____

MONDAY

TUESDAY

WEDNESDAY

THURSDAY

FRIDAY

COMPLETE TASK LIST

☐
☐
☐
☐
☐
☐
☐
☐
☐
☐
☐
☐
☐
☐
☐

NOTES

MUST-DO LIST

TEN-MINUTE TASKS

Phone Calls

Emails

Classrooms Check-Ins

Feedback and Follow-Up

Celebrations of Success

Positive Note

Positive Parent Connections

Self-Care Plan

Big Projects Ongoing or Upcoming

MY MONTHLY REFLECTIONS

ACCOMPLISHMENTS

WHAT WENT WELL

LESSONS LEARNED

WHAT TO CHANGE

Are there systems I can put in place that would make this month go smoother next year?

What is something I can simplify or do away with to improve this month next year?

DISTRICT LEADERSHIP MEETING COMMITMENTS

Use this tool to document commitments you or your building leadership team are making based on the work at this month's district leadership meeting.

Building leadership team meeting: _____ **Date:** _____

Commitments based on principal or building leadership team work:

Plan for next steps or work for building leadership team meeting:

Evidence of commitments:

End-of-Year Reflections

Self-reflection is critical. Just as you should review each day, week, and month, you should also set aside a block of time to review the year and reflect on it.

- Recognize your and your team's accomplishments and celebrate what went well.
- Reflect on lessons learned as well as on knowledge and skills acquired.
- Acknowledge mistakes and missteps so you can use them to improve.
- Analyze how you could do better next year.
- Think about what gives you joy and what you are passionate about.

As you consider the following end-of-year reflection prompts, ask yourself, "What evidence do I have that I'm a more effective leader now than I was a year ago?"

End-of-Year Reflection Prompts

A good way to review your year is to use some sentence stems to prompt your thinking, such as the following.

The most important goal I accomplished this year was . . .

_____

_____

These are the skills I acquired this year . . .

_____

_____

A big mistake I made this year—and the lesson I learned as a result—was . . .

_____

_____

An obstacle or challenge I overcame this year was . . .

_____

_____

Something I learned about other people was . . .

I laughed hard this year when . . .

The most fun I had this year was . . .

My best memory of the year was . . .

My biggest disappointment of the year was . . .

I adopted the new positive habit of . . .

I dropped the negative habit of . . .

My most common mental state this year was . . .

I grew emotionally this year by . . .

The nicest thing someone did for me this year was . . .

The nicest thing I did for someone else this year was . . .

If I could change one thing about this year, it would be . . .

One contribution I made to my community was . . .

This year I spent a lot of time . . .

_____

_____

This year I broke out of my comfort zone by . . .

_____

_____

My biggest time waster this year was . . .

_____

_____

I learned this great time-saving hack this year . . .

_____

_____

What I am most grateful for this year is . . .

_____

_____

These three words sum up this year . . .

_____

_____

If I could travel back to the beginning of the year, I would give myself this advice . . .

_____

_____

Reflection isn't the end of the process. Once you have reviewed and reflected, it's time to get ready for the year that will soon begin. The next school year is right around the corner!

LIVE YOUR BEST LIFE!

PART 3
Tools

PROJECT PLANNER

Use this tool to plan your projects from start to finish. If a project is an annual event, review the event when it's completed and add notes for next year. Even if a project does not happen again, there may be a similar future project; accurate notes help streamline future planning.

Project: _____ Date: _____ Due Date: _____

Overview:

Goal:

Success criteria:

Who needs to be at the table?

Task List

Task	Owner	Due Date	Completed

Items required to finish project:
☐
☐

Date of Completion: _____
☐
☐

Communication:

Notes for next year:

SETTING PROFESSIONAL AND PERSONAL GOALS

Putting a specific and measurable goal in writing helps to keep us focused on what we want to achieve. Often people set goals that are vague and unmeasurable. It's hard to know if your efforts are making a difference if you haven't identified the way you will measure success.

If you don't track your ongoing results, you won't know your progress, and if you don't track progress, you will quickly lose traction on achieving results. Imagine deciding that you want to lose thirty pounds in a year, and that you will do it by walking a mile a day and cutting sugar from your diet. But you never weigh yourself. It would be hard to stay motivated to continue your plan without seeing small successes along the way.

Equally important is identifying your motivation. If your purpose is strong enough, you will do whatever it takes to achieve it. You will commit to it. You will be constantly checking for success. You will adjust your actions when they are not working, and you will double down on what is working.

Achieving a goal does not always require big action. It may take small and consistent actions every single day. Success requires time. It also requires commitment.

In the "Goal-Setting Worksheet" (page 220), you will see two terms you might not be familiar with: (1) *lead measures* and (2) *lag measures*. The boxes on this page explain what they mean. The *lag measure* is the outcome you want to influence. Lag measures can't be directly changed, though; they are changed through the *lead measures*, or actions that you are going to take. The more specificity you include, the more effective your actions will be at achieving your goals.

Lag Measures	Lead Measures
Uncontrollable and unpredictable	Predictive and influenceable
Weight loss	Diet and exercise
Increased class engagement	Specific teacher feedback and targeted professional development
More students meeting standard on state assessment	Data and student work with targeted interventions based on the data

GOAL-SETTING WORKSHEET

Use this tool to set your personal goals and monitor your progress.

What is your motivation—the why?	What are your lead measures? (Things you control and can act on to improve the result.)
What are your lag measures? (Metrics you cannot control and cannot manage directly.)	Who needs to be a part of achieving this goal?
How will you measure success?	When, where, and how will you measure for success along the way?

What is the time frame for completion?

Check-In Date:

What data are you looking at? Are you moving toward hitting your goal?

Should you make any adjustments?

Check-In Date:
What data are you looking at? Have you achieved your goal?

DISTRICT LEADERSHIP MEETING COMMITMENTS

Use this tool to document commitments you or your building leadership team are making based on the work at this month's district leadership meeting.

Building leadership team meeting: _____ **Date:** _____

Commitments based on principal or building leadership team work:

Plan for next steps or work for building leadership team meeting:

Evidence of commitments:

"

Courage is needed not merely to launch the PLC journey but to sustain it. As William Faulkner writes, "You cannot swim for new horizons until you have the courage to lose sight of the shore." This courage, this willingness to leave the shore in pursuit of a better future, has been an essential attribute to America's success and prosperity. It took courage for the Pilgrims to leave their homes in pursuit of the New World. It took courage for settlers to harness a wagon and travel west in hopes of a better future. It took courage for three astronauts to board the Apollo 11 spacecraft, hoping to take a giant leap for mankind. Today the greatest generation of educators is being called on to summon the courage to take a giant leap of their own in order to secure a better life for our children and our nation.

So of every reader, I ask: "Do you believe it is desirable that schools function as PLCs? Do you believe that it is feasible that you and your colleagues can help your school become a high-performing PLC? Will you act with a sense of urgency, as if the very lives of your students depend on your action, because in a very literal sense, more so than at any other time in American history, they do?"

If your answer to these questions is "yes," then we must ask the most important question of all: "What are you personally prepared to do to bring the PLC process to life in your school or district?"

Thankfully, the greatest generation of American educators is on hand to take on this challenge.

—Richard DuFour

"

It is our sincere hope that this plan book helps you prioritize and lead the important work of improving the professional practice of your staff and improving learning for all students by implementing the concepts and practices of a PLC.

—Bob, Mike, Janel, and Meagan

References and Resources

Buffum, A., Mattos, M., & Malone, J. (2018). *Taking action: A handbook for RTI at Work*. Bloomington, IN: Solution Tree Press.

Conzemius, A. E., & O'Neill, J. (2014). *The handbook for SMART school teams: Revitalizing best practices for collaboration* (2nd ed.). Bloomington, IN: Solution Tree Press.

DuFour, R., DuFour, R., Eaker, R., & Karhanek, G. (2010). *Raising the bar and closing the gap: Whatever it takes*. Bloomington, IN: Solution Tree Press.

DuFour, R., DuFour, R., Eaker, R., & Many, T. (2006). *Learning by doing: A handbook for Professional Learning Communities at Work*. Bloomington, IN: Solution Tree Press.

DuFour, R., DuFour, R., Eaker, R., & Many, T. (2010). *Learning by doing: A handbook for Professional Learning Communities at Work* (2nd ed.). Bloomington, IN: Solution Tree Press.

DuFour, R., DuFour, R., Eaker, R., Many, T., & Mattos, M. (2016). *Learning by doing: A handbook for Professional Learning Communities at Work* (3rd ed.). Bloomington, IN: Solution Tree Press.

DuFour, R., & Eaker, R. (1998). *Professional Learning Communities at Work: Best practices for enhancing student achievement*. Bloomington, IN: Solution Tree Press.

Eaker, R., DuFour, R., & DuFour, R. (2002). *Getting started: Reculturing schools to become professional learning communities*. Bloomington, IN: Solution Tree Press.

Eaker, R., & Keating, J. (2008). A shift in school culture. *Journal of Staff Development, 29*(3), 14–17. Accessed at https://learningforward.org/wp-content/uploads/2008/06/A-Shift-In-School-Culture.pdf on May 4, 2020.

Eaker, R., Hagadone, M., Keating, J., & Rhoades, M. (2021). *Leading PLCs at Work districtwide: From boardroom to classroom*. Bloomington, IN: Solution Tree Press.

Eaker, R., & Sells, D. (2016). *A new way: Introducing higher education to Professional Learning Communities at Work*. Bloomington, IN: Solution Tree Press.

Eudaemonia. (n.d.). In Merriam-Webster's online dictionary. Accessed at https://merriam-webster.com/dictionary/eudaemonia on June 18, 2020.

Keating, J., & Rhoades, M. (2019, Fall). Stomping out PLC lite: Every school, every team. *AllThingsPLC Magazine*, 21–23.

Matthews, G. (2015). *Goals research summary*. Accessed at www.dominican.edu /sites/default/files/2020-02/gailmatthews-harvard-goals-researchsummary.pdf on September 10, 2019.

Owens, R. (1970). *Organizational behavior in schools*. Englewood Cliffs, NJ: Prentice-Hall.

Sharratt, G. (2002). *Keeping on your feet: A collection of stories*. Wenatchee, WA: North Central Educational Service District.

Sinek, S. (2009). *Start with why: How great leaders inspire everyone to take action*. New York: Portfolio.

"Tremendous, tremendous, tremendous!

The speaker made me do some very deep internal reflection about the **PLC process** and the personal responsibility I have in making the school improvement process work **for ALL kids**."

PD Services

Our experts draw from decades of research and their own experiences to bring you practical strategies for building and sustaining a high-performing PLC. You can choose from a range of customizable services, from a one-day overview to a multiyear process.

Book your PLC PD today!
888.763.9045

Solution Tree

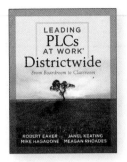

Leading PLCs at Work® Districtwide
Robert Eaker, Mike Hagadone, Janel Keating, and Meagan Rhoades
Ensure your district is doing the right work, the right way, for the right reasons. With this resource as your guide, you will learn how to align the work of every PLC team districtwide—from the boardroom to the classroom.
BKF942

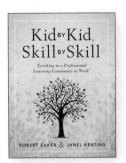

Kid by Kid, Skill by Skill
Robert Eaker and Janel Keating
This book explores professional learning communities from a teacher's perspective. Focused chapters survey effective and collaborative team actions, instructional practices that enhance teacher efficiency, and the role teacher judgment and classroom context play in determining instructional outcomes.
BKF694

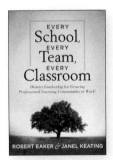

Every School, Every Team, Every Classroom
Robert Eaker and Janel Keating
The PLC journey begins with a dedication to ensuring the learning of every student. Using many examples and reproducible tools, the authors explain the need to focus on creating simultaneous top-down and bottom-up leadership. Learn how to grow PLCs by encouraging innovation at every level.
BKF534

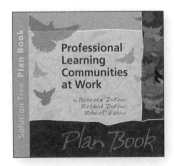

Professional Learning Communities at Work® Plan Book
Rebecca DuFour, Richard DuFour, and Robert Eaker
Teachers love this plan book! This great organizer, with forty weekly planning pages and space for eight class periods, is also a process book packed with creative ideas, activities, and inspirational success stories that address crucial, teacher-specific PLC concepts.
BKF217